GETTING TO KNOW
THE U.S. PRESIDENTS

C A L V I N
COOLIDGE

THIRTIETH PRESIDENT
1923 – 1929

WRITTEN AND ILLUSTRATED BY MIKE VENEZIA

CHILDREN'S PRES
A DIVISION OF SCHOLASTIC
NEW YORK   TORONTO   LONDON   AUCKLAND   SYDNEY
MEXICO CITY   NEW DELHI   HONG KONG
DANBURY, CONNECTICUT

PAULINE HAASS PUBLIC LIBRARY

Reading Consultant: Nanci R. Vargus, Ed.D., Assistant Professor, School of Education, University of Indianapolis

Historical Consultant: Marc J. Selverstone, Ph.D., Assistant Professor, Miller Center of Public Affairs, University of Virginia

Photographs © 2007: AP/Wide World Photos: 30 top, 30 bottom, 32; Bridgeman Art Library International Ltd., London/New York/Private Collection/Archives Charmet: 28; Brown Brothers: 13; Calvin Coolidge Memorial Foundation: 6; Corbis Images: 3, 22, 24 left (Bettmann), 24 right (David J. & Janice L. Frent Collection), 10 (Lake County Museum); Forbes Library, Northhampton, MA: 17, 18; Grandma Moses Properties Co., New York/Private Collection, courtesy of Gallerie St. Etienne, New York: 8; Historic Northampton, Northampton, MA: 16; Library of Congress: 21; The Image Works/Topham/Roger-Voillet: 25; Vermont Division for Historic Preservation, President Calvin Coolidge State Historic Site: 26.

Colorist for illustrations: Dave Ludwig

Library of Congress Cataloging-in-Publication Data

Venezia, Mike.
   Calvin Coolidge / written and illustrated by Mike Venezia.
      p. cm. — (Getting to know the U.S. presidents)
   ISBN-10:   0-516-22634-7 (lib. bdg.)   0-516-25210-0 (pbk.)
   ISBN-13:   978-0-516-22634-7 (lib. bdg.)   978-0-516-25210-0 (pbk.)
   1.   Coolidge, Calvin, 1872-1933—Juvenile literature. 2.
Presidents—United States—Biography—Juvenile literature.   I. Title.
   E792.V46 2007
   973.91'5092-dc22   2006000456

Copyright 2007 by Mike Venezia.
All rights reserved. Published in 2007 by Children's Press, an imprint
of Scholastic Library Publishing. Published simultaneously in Canada.
Printed in The United States of America.

CHILDREN'S PRESS and associated logos are trademarks
and/or registered trademarks of Scholastic Library Publishing.
SCHOLASTIC and associated logos are trademarks and/or
registered trademarks of Scholastic Inc.

1 2 3 4 5 6 7 8 9 10 R 16 15 14 13 12 11 10 09 08 07

A photograph of President Calvin Coolidge

Calvin Coolidge was the thirtieth president of the United States. He was born on July 4, 1872, in Plymouth Notch, Vermont. Calvin was always on the shy side. Even after he became president, Calvin didn't speak very much. Because of his quiet behavior, he was known as "Silent Cal."

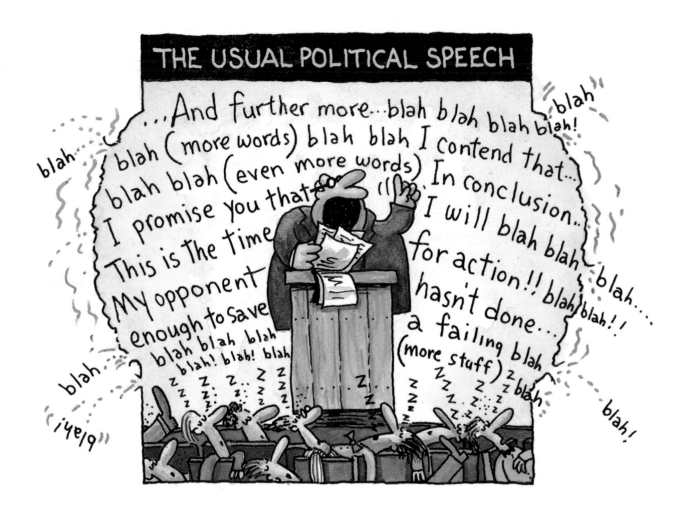

Calvin Coolidge didn't believe in wasting words. While some politicians gave speeches that lasted for hours, Calvin's speeches sometimes lasted only a few minutes. People seemed to like Calvin's direct, no-nonsense comments. Calvin didn't believe in wasting money, either.

When he was president, Calvin wore medium-priced suits and hated big, fancy dinner parties. He never accepted expensive gifts from people, either. Even though Calvin was just handling his money carefully, some people accused him or being a cheapskate.

Calvin Coolidge at about the age of seven

Calvin Coolidge learned a lot of his behavior from his parents and the people who lived in Plymouth Notch. His father ran a small grocery store and was also a farmer. The land in the area was rocky and very difficult to farm. Instead of becoming discouraged, however, people in Vermont were thankful for the smallest things.

The Coolidges and their neighbors got along with very little and were used to saving every penny. They hardly ever complained, either. Mr. Coolidge taught Calvin that helping others and being a public servant was also an important part of life.

Bringing in the Maple Sugar, by Grandma Moses. 1939 or earlier, oil on pressed wood, 14 x 22 in. © Grandma Moses Properties Co., New York/Private Collection, courtesy of Galerie St. Etienne, New York.

Calvin was never late or absent from school, but he was just a so-so student. As a boy, he spent most of his time doing farm chores. Calvin was a good worker, especially when it came time to gather sap from maple trees. Maple sap is used to make sugar and syrup.

While growing up, Calvin enjoyed making his own bow, arrows, and kites. Calvin liked hunting, fishing, and ice-skating, too. Calvin was always a serious boy, but he did pick up a clever sense of humor from his grandfather. Grandpa Coolidge also taught Calvin horseback-riding tricks.

The library at Amherst College

When Calvin was thirteen years old, his father enrolled him in a nearby academy. Calvin was just an average student there, too. When it came time to go to college, though, Calvin worked really hard to pass the entrance exam for Amherst College in Massachusetts.

Calvin started out at Amherst in his usual shy way. He found it hard to make friends at his new school. Instead of trying out for

sports or going to parties, Calvin preferred
walking through the woods by himself.
Then something happened that changed
Calvin. An excellent teacher inspired him.
Mr. Garman convinced his students to have
confidence in their thoughts and beliefs.
He encouraged them to use their talents to
help others.

Calvin Coolidge made up his mind to fight his shyness. He knew he'd have to be friendlier and talk more if he wanted to help people someday. Calvin joined a political club and helped support President Benjamin Harrison when it was time for the next election. Slowly, Calvin became more sure of himself.

Calvin Coolidge while he was a student at Amherst College

Calvin gained even more confidence when he was asked to give a last-minute speech at his school. Calvin surprised himself. His speech got lots of laughs and applause from a large group of students. Calvin discovered that people really enjoyed his special sense of humor.

Calvin graduated from Amherst College in 1895. He told his father he was determined to do some good in the world. Calvin decided the best way to start would be to become a lawyer. He moved to the town of Northampton, Massachusetts, where he got a job as a clerk in a law office.

Calvin studied there until he was able to pass his law exam. He became a lawyer in 1897 and opened up his own office in Northampton. Since he preferred to do everything himself, without help, Calvin was busier than ever.

Northampton, Massachusetts, in the early 1900s

Calvin Coolidge did manage to find time to join the state's Republican Party. He worked hard to get Republican candidates elected to different government jobs. Soon Calvin became known as a dependable and loyal party member.

Calvin Coolidge as a young lawyer in Northampton

In 1899, Calvin ran for political office himself. He was elected to the Northampton town council. It was the beginning of a successful political career. Calvin Coolidge slowly moved up to higher and higher elected positions throughout his life. He still managed to keep his law business going, and even found time to get married.

Calvin Coolidge and his wife Grace

Calvin met his future wife in 1904. Grace Goodhue was a teacher at the Clark Institute for the Deaf, which was next door to Calvin's boarding house. Townspeople thought they made a strange couple. Grace was lively, charming, and loved to have fun at parties. Calvin was the same as he had always been, silent and not interested in parties at all.

For some reason, the two were crazy about each other. Calvin and Grace got married in 1905. They ended up having two sons. Grace was the perfect wife for Calvin. She always knew just how to handle her husband's penny-pinching ways and stubborn moods.

Calvin soon put more effort into getting elected to different government jobs. He was elected to the Massachusetts House of Representatives, and then he became mayor of Northampton. A few years later, Calvin was elected a state senator, lieutenant governor of Massachusetts, and finally, governor of the state. Calvin did a fine job in all of his positions. It was during the time he was governor, though, that Calvin became known across the country for an important decision he made.

Governor Calvin Coolidge

Guardsmen protecting a looted store during the 1919 Boston Police Strike

In 1919, policemen in Boston, Massachusetts, went on strike. They were tired of getting low pay. As soon as they stopped working, mobs of crooks and thieves broke into stores and took whatever they wanted. The mayor of Boston and Governor Coolidge sent in armed soldiers to protect the city. Governor Coolidge was so angry he wanted all striking policemen to be fired.

Even though Calvin agreed that the police officers weren't being paid enough, he said that no one had the right to risk the public's safety anywhere, anytime, ever! People across the United States were impressed with Calvin's feelings about law and order.

UNDER
The 19th
Amendment
I CAST MY
FIRST VOTE
Nov. 2nd, 1920

Harding
Coolidge

The Straight
Republican
Ticket

Lancaster, Pa.

In 1920, the Republican Party nominated Warren G. Harding for president and Calvin Coolidge for vice president.

When it was time for the election of 1920, some Republicans thought Calvin Coolidge should run for president. As it turned out, Calvin wasn't chosen for president, but was picked to run for vice president. Calvin teamed up with Warren G. Harding, the Republican candidate for president.

Harding and Coolidge easily won the election that year. Calvin, Grace, and their two sons left Massachusetts and moved to Washington, D.C. Calvin wasn't vice president for long, though. Just about halfway through his first term, President Harding died unexpectedly.

Calvin Coolidge with his wife and sons

This illustration shows Calvin Coolidge being sworn in as president by his father.

Calvin Coolidge was on vacation visiting his father when he got the news. Because Calvin's father was a justice of the peace, he was able to swear in Calvin as president. Calvin Coolidge suddenly became president of the United States on August 3, 1923.

As soon as Calvin got back to Washington, D.C., he found that President Harding had left things in quite a mess. President Harding had appointed many of his friends to important government positions. Some of these friends had made dishonest deals and had stolen government money for themselves. People were furious when they found out. Because President Coolidge was known as an honest and fair man, the public trusted him to straighten out the mess. President Coolidge worked quickly to replace corrupt workers with honest, respectable men.

Before he knew it, it was time for President Coolidge to campaign for the next election. Calvin easily won the election of 1924. People admired the honest, plainspoken, easy-going president. They liked the way President Coolidge kept the government from making rules and regulations to control big business.

An Assembly Line
of the
Ford Motor Company

Auto manufacturing was one of many American industries that were booming in the 1920s.

President Coolidge wanted companies and factories to be able to grow freely and make as much money as possible, without the government telling them how to do it. Because of this, many people in the United States had jobs and made a good living. Not everyone was fortunate, though. Farmers were having an especially hard time selling their crops. Many farmers could hardly keep their farms running. President Coolidge could have helped them, but decided the government should stay out of the farming business, too. Calvin Coolidge believed by leaving things alone, most problems in the United States would work themselves out naturally.

President Coolidge clad in cowboy attire during a Fourth of July celebration in North Dakota

It's true that President Coolidge preferred to speak as little as possible at social events. But Calvin could talk quite a lot if necessary. He frequently held press conferences to let people know how the country was doing.

President Coolidge was also a good sport.

He was always willing to pose for newspaper photographers. Sometimes he'd wear cowboy hats or full Indian headdresses.

President Coolidge poses in a traditional feathered headdress given to him by Sioux Indians at the "Days of 1876" celebration in Deadwood, South Dakota.

For exercise, Calvin had a mechanical horse installed in the White House. Visitors were surprised to find the president whooping and waving a cowboy hat while riding the machine! The Coolidges loved pets and let their dog, cat, and pet raccoon run freely around the White House.

Calvin Coolidge fishing during his retirement

President Coolidge could have run for another four-year term in 1928, but surprised everyone by announcing at the last minute that he wasn't interested. He never gave a reason for his decision. Some historians believe the president was having health problems.

Another reason might have been that he was just too sad to continue being president. During the election of 1924, Calvin and Grace's son, Calvin, Jr., had died of a blood infection. In the 1920s there were no medications to save his life. When Calvin's term ended, the family returned to their home in Northampton. Only four years later, in 1933, Calvin died there at the age of sixty.

PAULINE HAASS PUBLIC LIBRARY
N64 W23820 MAIN STREET
SUSSEX, WISCONSIN 53089
(262) 246-5180   9/07